I0846495

MURDER IN PLAIN SIGHT

Domestic Abuse: The Death Of The Modern Woman

Maya Angelo

@Copyright 2023 by Maya Angelo

All rights reserved.

No portion of this book may be reproduce, distributed or transmitted in any form without written permission from the author or publisher, except as permitted by U.S copyright law.

DEDICATION

This book is dedicated to all victims of Domestic violence, both survivors and those who died in the fight. Your fight was not in vain, for those still struggling, you will overcome.

Table of Contents:

INTRODUCTIONS

Domestic abuse, known as "intimate partner violence," involves a repetitive pattern of behavior aimed at gaining power and control over an intimate partner. It encompasses various forms such as physical, sexual, emotional, economic, or psychological actions, which can intimidate, manipulate, hurt, or humiliate the victim. This kind of abuse is not limited by race, age, sexual orientation, religion, or gender and can occur within married, cohabiting, or dating couples. It affects individuals from different socioeconomic backgrounds and education levels.

Victims of domestic abuse may include not only the intimate partner but also children, relatives, or other household members. This abuse is characterized by an ongoing abusive behavior pattern by the abuser towards their intimate partner, and it can take various forms such as mental, physical, economic, or sexual abuse. Incidents rarely remain isolated; instead, they tend to escalate in frequency and severity, sometimes leading to severe physical injuries or even death.

Do you suspect you might be experiencing abuse in your relationship? Reflect on the following questions to evaluate how you are being treated and how you treat your partner:

Identifying signs of domestic abuse:

- Does your partner mock or embarrass you in front of friends or family?
- Do they belittle your accomplishments?
- Are you made to feel incapable of making decisions?
- Does your partner use intimidation or threats to make you comply?
- Have they told you that you are worthless without them?
- Do they physically harm you, such as grabbing, pushing, pinching, shoving, or hitting?
- Does your partner excessively call you or show up uninvited to check your whereabouts?
- Have drugs or alcohol been used as an excuse for hurtful behavior or abuse?
- Are you blamed for your partner's emotions or actions?
- Have you been pressured sexually for things you aren't ready for?

- Do you feel trapped in the relationship, with no way out?
- Are you prevented from doing things you enjoy, like spending time with friends or family?
- Has your partner tried to restrain you after a fight or left you somewhere as a form of punishment?

CONSIDER IF YOU...

- Feel afraid of your partner's potential behavior at times.
- Find yourself constantly making excuses for your partner's actions to others.
- Believe that you can change your partner if you change something about yourself.
- Avoid doing anything that may cause conflict or anger in your partner.
- Prioritize your partner's wishes over your own desires.
- Stay in the relationship out of fear of what your partner might do if you were to break up.

If any of these situations resonate with you, it's essential to talk to someone about it. Seeking help is crucial, as abuse can persist without intervention. Making that initial call for support requires courage, but it's a vital step towards breaking free from abuse.

WHY LEAVING IS NECESSARY

It's important to grasp that abuse is primarily about control, and abusers employ various manipulative tactics to dominate their partners, who are essentially victims in this situation. True partners are equals who love and respect each other, something abusers are incapable of doing.

Additionally, it's crucial to acknowledge that there's nothing you can do to change or fix an abusive person. No amount of love or compassion will be enough, as they perceive these qualities as weaknesses and will exploit them further if you try to help. Understanding this dynamic, accepting that things won't improve, and taking action to remove yourself from the abusive relationship is imperative.

Abusers possess the ability to control themselves but deliberately choose not to when it comes to the person closest to them, whom they claim to love. They pick and choose whom to abuse, saving their mistreatment for those they claim to be in a loving relationship with. Abusers carefully plan when and where to be abusive, ensuring their behavior remains hidden from others. They can cease their abusive actions when it benefits them, demonstrating that they are not entirely out of control. In cases of physical violence, abusers often target areas that won't display visible marks to conceal their actions.

If you closely examine your dating relationship, you might discover how abusers deliberately selected and manipulated you, creating a false persona to charm not only you but also your friends and family. Abusers can be charismatic and seemingly perfect partners initially, sweeping you off your feet until you realize the facade. By then, they've worn you down, made you doubt yourself, and convinced you that you are the problem.

ABUSERS UTILIZE VARIOUS TACTICS TO EXERT POWER AND CONTROL:

1. Dominance: Treating you as inferior and making decisions for you, creating a sense of ownership.

2. Humiliation: Constantly belittling and insulting you to erode your self-esteem.

3. Isolation: Cutting you off from support systems to increase dependence on them.

4. Threats: Using intimidation and threats to instill fear and maintain control.

5. Intimidation: Displaying violent behavior or gestures to scare and control you.

6. Denial and blame: Excusing their abusive actions or placing the blame on you.

Staying in an abusive relationship can have severe consequences, leading to anxiety, depression, health issues, and feelings of hopelessness. It can erode your self-worth and happiness, preventing you from living a fulfilling life with a loving and respectful partner. Remember, you have the power to choose how you want to live your life.

If you still love the abuser or feel pressured to stay due to external factors, the decision ultimately lies with you. Seek help and support from domestic hotlines, shelters, or the police if needed, and remember that your life and well-being are of utmost importance.

CHAPTER TWO
RECOGNIZING THE SIGNS OF DOMESTIC VIOLENCE

The most evident forms of domestic abuse and violence are physical and sexual assaults or threats to commit them. These actions often draw attention to the problem. However, an abuser's regular use of other abusive behaviors, combined with occasional physical violence, forms a broader system of abuse. Even if physical assaults occur infrequently, they create fear of future attacks, granting the abuser control over the victim's life and situation. The following outlines various types of domestic abuse and ways to recognize them.

Emotional abuse encompasses actions that undermine a person's self-worth, such as constant criticism, belittling, name-calling, or isolating them from loved ones. Signs of emotional abuse in a relationship may include:

EMOTIONAL ABUSE
- Verbal insults, name-calling, or continuous criticism.

- Lack of trust and possessive behavior.

- Attempting to isolate you from family and friends.

- Monitoring your activities, calls, and interactions.

- Prohibiting you from working or controlling finances.

- Withholding affection as punishment.

- Expecting you to ask for permission.

- Threatening harm to you, your children, family, or pets.

- Humiliating you in various ways.

PSYCHOLOGICAL ABUSE

Psychological abuse instills fear through intimidation, threats of physical harm to oneself, the partner, or the children, destruction of property, and forcing isolation from support systems like friends, family, school, or work.

FINANCIAL ABUSE

Financial or economic abuse involves making someone financially dependent by controlling all financial resources, restricting access to money, or forbidding education or employment opportunities.

PHYSICAL ABUSE

Physical abuse involves harming a partner through physical force, such as hitting, kicking, burning, grabbing, slapping, hair-pulling, or denying medical care. Signs of physical abuse include:

- Damaging property during anger outbursts.

- Physical violence like pushing, slapping, biting, or choking.

- Abandoning you in dangerous situations.

- Driving recklessly to scare you.

- Threatening or using weapons against you.

- Forcing you to leave your home or keeping you trapped.

- Preventing you from seeking help or medical attention.

- Harming your children.

- Using physical force during sexual encounters.

In cases of physical abuse, the individual is likely to exhibit frequent bruises or injuries that align with being punched, choked, or knocked down, and their explanations for these injuries are often weak or inconsistent.

It is frequent for individuals experiencing domestic abuse to attempt to conceal the physical signs by wearing clothing that covers the affected areas. For instance, someone you care about might wear long sleeves or scarves even in hot weather. Other common signs include

wearing heavier makeup than usual or wearing
sunglasses indoors to hide injuries or bruises.

SEXUAL ABUSE

Sexual abuse entails coercing a partner into participating
in sexual activities without their consent. Signs of a
sexually abusive relationship may include:

- Accusing you of cheating or displaying frequent
  jealousy towards your outside relationships.
- Pressuring you to dress in a sexual manner.
- Insulting you with sexual remarks or names.
- Forcing or manipulating you into engaging in
  sexual acts.
- Using physical force during sex, such as holding
  you down.
- Demanding sex when you are unwell, exhausted,
  or after abusing you.
- Inflicting harm using weapons or objects during
  sexual encounters.
- Involving other people in sexual activities without
  your consent.
- Ignoring your feelings and boundaries regarding
  sex.

STALKING

Stalking involves repeated patterns of behavior with no legitimate purpose, aiming to harass, annoy, or terrify the victim. Typical stalking actions include frequent phone calls, unsolicited letters or gifts, and surveillance at home, work, or other frequented places. Stalking often escalates over time.

THE CIRCLE OF ABUSE

The cycle of abuse typically involves four primary stages: tension, incident, reconciliation, and calm. While abusive behaviors may escalate from one cycle to another, it doesn't occur in all cases of abuse, which can add to the pain and confusion.

Abuse varies from person to person and situation to situation. Even within the same relationship, abusive behaviors can fluctuate over time, and at times, they might seem to stop before resurfacing. This pattern is commonly known as the cycle of abuse.

Psychologists have extensively observed and interviewed women who have encountered abuse and domestic violence, leading them to identify several recurring stages in an abusive relationship.

These stages in the cycle of abuse include:

1. Tension building

2. Incident of violence

3. Reconciliation

4. Calm

While mental health professionals have utilized this model as a reference, it's essential to note that it may not encompass all experiences related to abuse.

TENSION BUILDING

During the tension-building stage, the abusive partner may exhibit abusive behaviors that gradually intensify and become more frequent. This escalation could be triggered by external stressors like financial troubles, work-related challenges, or health issues.

The growing tension may manifest as emotional outbursts, irritability, impatience, and a short temper. As the outside world feels increasingly uncontrollable, the abusive person may seek to regain a sense of control through their relationship.

As the tension becomes more apparent, the non-abusive partner may also experience increasing anxiety. In response, they may adopt specific behaviors, like "walking on eggshells," to ease the tense situation and pacify the abusive partner, attempting to prevent any abusive incidents.

INCIDENT

As the tension from the initial stage in the cycle of abuse begins to subside, one or more abusive incidents may occur. During this stage, the abusive partner makes overt attempts to regain a sense of power and control.

Abusive incidents can vary in appearance, both from one instance to another and from one relationship to another. They may involve intimidation, threats of violence, breaking of household items, verbal abuse like insults and name-calling, physical violence, sexual violence, shaming, blaming, manipulation tactics like the silent treatment or gaslighting, humiliation, social isolation, financial abuse, and emotional abandonment.

With each cycle, it is possible for the incident stage to escalate. For instance, the early cycles may involve intimidation and insults, while physical violence may become more prominent as the relationship progresses.

RECONCILLIATION

Following the incident of abuse, the abusive partner may feel a sense of relief as the tension begins to dissipate.

However, the experience for the victim of the abuse can be quite different.

With the tension eased, the abusive partner may try to make amends by apologizing, showing affection, or making promises to change. They might genuinely appear ashamed of their behavior and committed to improving. As the victim cares about them, they may be tempted to believe these efforts and offer another chance.

During the reconciliation stage, the abusive partner may engage in romantic, supportive, and loving behaviors to create a sense of calm. However, as this phase progresses, you may notice a shift in their approach. They might start excusing their actions, minimizing the abusive behaviors, or blaming external factors for their conduct.

CALM STAGE

In the calm phase, your partner may still be attentive, but you might notice a shift in their behavior from being apologetic to now finding excuses for their actions.

During this stage, abusive behaviors may be downplayed, and you may observe your partner:

- Shifting responsibility for the abuse, saying things like "I'm sorry, but it's all because of so-and-so."

- Justifying their behavior, claiming "If the garbage man didn't do that, I wouldn't get so angry."

- Gaslighting you by dismissing the severity of their actions, saying "It really wasn't that big of a deal."

This stage can be perplexing because your partner initially appeared remorseful and eager to make amends, but now there's an underlying tone of dismissal that you can't quite pinpoint. As time passes, you may start to feel the tension building again as the cycle of abuse repeats once more.

Some individuals may wonder why their emotionally abusive boyfriend sometimes acts affectionate and loving. This behavior is referred to as "love bombing," where the abuser showers affection to regain control after realizing the abuse has gone too far. Both the abuse and love bombing are methods of control. Unfortunately, the abuse tends to escalate, with the abuser continuously shifting the goalposts for what they consider as "too far." The love bombing may eventually vanish, leading to constant stress and tiptoeing around the abuser's moods.

It's essential to break free from such a toxic relationship and prioritize your well-being.

The abuse is continuous, and the moments of sweetness are an integral part of it. These acts of kindness make it difficult for you to leave, causing confusion and guilt when confronted with the overtly abusive behaviors. The abuser never ceases to be abusive.

CHAPTER THREE

SAFETY PLANNING

A safety plan is a personalized and practical strategy designed to enhance your safety while dealing with abuse, preparing to leave an abusive situation, or after you have left. This plan is customized to suit your specific circumstances and includes crucial information to help you prepare for and handle various scenarios. It covers aspects like informing friends and family about your situation, managing emotions, and accessing resources that cater to your individual needs.

Even though some preparations for a safety plan might seem obvious, it can be challenging to think clearly or make rational decisions during moments of crisis. Having a safety plan already established can aid in protecting yourself and others during high-stress situations.

The following safety planning resources offer essential guidance for creating a safety plan. They are valuable for survivors, friends, family members, or anyone concerned about their safety or the safety of others involved in an abusive situation.

PHYSICAL SAFETY PLAN

Living with an abusive partner can make it challenging to recognize opportunities to leave. Here are crucial steps for safety planning while in such a situation:

1. Assess your partner's use and level of force to gauge the risk of physical danger for yourself and others before it escalates.

2. Identify safe areas in your home with clear pathways to exit, away from any weapons. If arguments arise, try moving to these areas before the situation escalates.

3. Always keep a phone accessible and know important numbers to call for help, such as friends, family, emergency hotline and your local shelter. Know the nearest public phone location.

4. Inform trusted friends and neighbors about your situation and establish a plan and visual signal for when you may need their assistance. Specify who they should and should not contact during crises, including law enforcement.

5. Discuss getting help with others in the residence, such as children or roommates. Advise them not to intervene in the violence between you and your partner and create a mutual signal for when they should seek help or leave the house.

6. Plan plausible reasons for leaving the house at different times of the day or night, such as multiple trips to the grocery store, spending time with friends, or staying at work longer. Find unnecessary errands to run.

7. Practice safe ways to leave, if possible, including involving others living in the residence.

8. Develop a plan for if your partner discovers your intentions to leave.

9. Keep weapons, like guns and knives, locked away and stored out of reach. If you feel unsafe, reach out to an Advocate for support.

10. Be mindful of how clothing or jewelry could be used to harm you physically, especially if your partner has previously put their hands around your neck.

11. Back your car into the driveway when parking at home and keep it fueled. If possible, keep the driver's door unlocked while locking the rest of the doors for quick access to the vehicle.

12. If violence becomes unavoidable, try to make yourself as small as possible. Move to a corner, curl into a ball, protect your face, and wrap your arms around your head with fingers entwined

SAFETY MEASURES WITH KIDS

Ensure that your safety plan includes measures to keep your children safe during violent situations and important considerations while preparing to leave and afterward.

Safety measures at home:

1. Educate your children on when, how, and whom to contact in emergencies, such as trusted friends, family, neighbors, and local service providers.

2. If possible, instruct them to leave the home when situations begin to escalate and have a predetermined safe place they can go to with trusted individuals during a crisis.

3. Establish a secret code word for emergency situations, and ensure they understand not to disclose its meaning to others.

4. Designate a specific room in the house for them to seek refuge when afraid and provide something calming for them to focus on for comfort.

5. Instruct them to stay away from areas that may contain items potentially used to harm them, like kitchens and bathrooms.

6. Teach them not to intervene during violent moments, even though they may want to protect their parents.

7. Plan for contingencies if your children inform your partner about your leaving plan and always avoid blaming them for their responses to your partner's abusive behavior.

SAFETY MEASURES WITH PREGNANCY

Pregnancy is a period characterized by intense emotions, both positive and negative, which often requires additional support from those around you. It is natural to rely on emotional and financial assistance from a partner during this time to prepare for the baby. However, if your partner is emotionally or physically abusive, this transitional period can become particularly difficult and unsafe. Abuse may begin or worsen during pregnancy, making it crucial to create a safety plan.

Pregnancy is the second most dangerous time in an abusive relationship.

If you are concerned about your safety, please seek help from an advocate or develop a safety plan.

Seeking help while pregnant:

1. Doctor's visits can be an opportunity to discuss your situation and plan to leave if you have decided to do so.

2. If your partner accompanies you to doctor's appointments, try to find a moment alone with your healthcare provider or the front desk receptionist to seek their help.

3. Consider attending prenatal classes that only include those giving birth, as this environment may provide a comfortable space to discuss pregnancy concerns or speak privately with the instructor.

4. Be aware of the heightened risk during violent situations while pregnant. If you live in a multi-level home, try to stay on the first floor to avoid potential harm. If violence becomes unavoidable and you cannot escape, assume the fetal position and protect your stomach with your arms.

At the end, LEAVE! Don't compromise on it, your life is at risk.

I usually get questions like "how can I ensure my safety after leaving an abusive relationship?"

At the very least, consider relocating from the area where you are with your abuser. Inform everyone not to disclose any information about your whereabouts. The level of possessiveness displayed by your abuser will determine the necessary measures to take. Evaluate the threat and comprehend the abuser's potential actions to determine your course of action. Additionally, seek assistance from organizations that can guide you through legal steps.

OBTAINING RESOURCES AND BUILDING SUPPORT

Securing resources and support is a crucial step in ensuring your safety and well-being as you navigate an abusive relationship. This phase involves reaching out to various sources of assistance and building a network of support to help you during this challenging time. Here are the key elements to consider when seeking resources and support:

1. Reach Out to Trusted Individuals: Connect with people you trust, such as friends, family, or colleagues, and confide in them about your situation. Sharing your

experiences with them can provide valuable emotional support and understanding.

2. Seek Professional Help: Reach out to mental health professionals, counselors, therapists, or support groups that specialize in domestic abuse. They can offer guidance, coping strategies, and a safe environment to share your feelings.

3. Contact Domestic Violence Hotlines: Get in touch with local or national domestic violence hotlines that offer confidential support and information. Trained advocates can provide advice, resources, and safety planning tailored to your specific circumstances.

4. Consult Legal Assistance: If necessary, seek advice from an attorney or legal aid organization to explore legal options such as restraining orders, custody arrangements, or divorce proceedings. Understanding your rights and navigating the legal process is essential.

5. Assess Financial Support: Evaluate your financial situation and explore available resources, including government assistance programs, shelters, or nonprofit organizations that offer financial aid to survivors of domestic abuse.

6. Connect with Supportive Organizations: Research and connect with local organizations that specialize in supporting survivors of domestic abuse. They often provide services like emergency shelter, counseling, legal assistance, and support groups.

7. Develop a Safety Plan: Collaborate with professionals or organizations to create a comprehensive safety plan tailored to your circumstances. This plan outlines steps to take in emergencies, identifies safe spaces, and minimizes risk.

8. Seek Medical Attention: If you've experienced physical harm, seek medical attention and discuss your situation with healthcare providers. They can document injuries, provide necessary care, and refer you to resources.

9. Work Towards Financial Independence: If possible, take steps to achieve financial independence by saving money, securing employment, or accessing financial resources to transition to a safer environment.

10. Counseling for Children: If you have children, consider counseling or therapy services for them to address any emotional or psychological impact they may have experienced due to the abusive relationship.

11. Educate Yourself: Attend workshops, seminars, or training sessions provided by organizations that focus on domestic abuse. These educational opportunities can empower you with knowledge about healthy relationships, boundaries, and personal growth.

Remember, securing resources and support is a gradual process that requires careful planning and persistence. Reach out to professionals and organizations specialized in assisting survivors of domestic abuse to create a comprehensive support network that prioritizes your safety and well-being.

CHAPTER FOUR

UNDERSTANDING THE LEGAL ASPECTS

OBTAINING A RESTRAINING ORDER

A restraining order, also known as a "protective order," is a legal court order designed to protect an individual from physical or sexual abuse, threats, stalking, or harassment. The person who receives the restraining order is referred to as the "protected person," while the person against whom the order is issued is the "restrained person." In some cases, the order may also extend protection to other "protected persons," such as family or household members of the individual seeking protection.

A RESTRAINING ORDER CAN ENCOMPASS VARIOUS PROVISIONS, INCLUDING:

1. Personal Conduct Orders: These orders prohibit specific acts against all individuals named as "protected persons" in the restraining order. Such acts may include contacting, calling, or sending messages (including e-mail); attacking, striking, or battering; stalking; threatening; sexually assaulting; harassing; destroying

personal property; or disturbing the peace of the protected individuals.

2. Stay-Away Orders: These orders mandate that the restrained person stay a certain distance away (e.g., 50 or 100 yards) from the protected person or persons, the protected person's residence, workplace, children's schools or places of child care, vehicle, and other significant places they frequent.

3. Residence Exclusion ("Kick-Out" or "Move-Out") Orders: These orders direct the restrained person to vacate the residence where the protected person lives and take only clothing and personal belongings until the court hearing. Such orders are typically sought in cases involving domestic violence or abuse of elderly or dependent adults.

For the restrained person, having a restraining order against them can lead to severe consequences:

1. Restricted Access: The restrained person may be barred from specific places or activities.

2. Eviction: They might be required to move out of their home.

3. Limited Child Custody: Their ability to see their children may be affected.

4. Firearms Restrictions: Generally, the restrained person will be prohibited from owning a gun, and they must surrender, sell, or store any guns they currently possess while the restraining order is in effect.

5. Immigration Implications: If the restrained person is seeking a green card or visa, the restraining order may impact their immigration status.

Furthermore, violating the restraining order can result in imprisonment, fines, or both for the restrained person.

There are four different types of restraining orders that you can request:

1. Domestic Violence Restraining Order
2. Elder or Dependent Adult Abuse Restraining Order
3. Civil Harassment Restraining Order
4. Workplace Violence Restraining Order

We are going to talk about number one which is domestic violence restraining order

You may request a domestic violence restraining order under the following circumstances:

1. If someone has subjected you to abuse, and

2. You share a close relationship with that individual (e.g., married or registered domestic partners, divorced, separated, dating or used to date, have a child together, or live together or used to live together etc), or you are closely related (parent, child, brother, sister, grandmother, grandfather, in-law).
On these grounds, you are eligible for a restraining order against your spouse

If you're considering obtaining a restraining or protective order, it's essential to know the laws in your state and the specific procedure involved. Reach out to the district attorney's office, and when signing the affidavit, be truthful and provide solid evidence to back up your claims.

In some cases, like when a person is arrested for attacking you, the court may automatically issue a restraining order. However, don't solely rely on temporary orders; gather as much evidence as possible, such as police reports, hospital records, and photographs of injuries, to strengthen your case.

Remember, hearsay is not accepted in court, so make sure to have direct witnesses who can testify to what happened. Abusers often deny their actions, so having concrete evidence is vital. Be prepared for the court hearing, as the accused will have a chance to present their side of the story.

Getting a restraining order might not be easy, but if you have solid proof of threats or harm, it can make a significant difference. Build a strong safety plan, collect evidence, and seek legal advice to ensure your well-being and protection.

WORKING WITH LAW ENFORCEMENT

Working with law enforcement can be a crucial step in addressing domestic abuse and seeking protection. Police officers are trained to respond to emergency situations, and their involvement can help ensure your safety and provide legal avenues for pursuing justice. Here's a more in-depth look at working with law enforcement:

1. Emergency Response: If you are in immediate danger, call the emergency number to report the abuse. Police officers will respond promptly to protect you from harm and assess the situation. Provide as much information as possible about the abusive incident, including details

about the abuser, any weapons involved, and any threats made.

2. Gathering Evidence: When the police arrive, cooperate fully and provide a detailed account of what happened. Be honest and provide any evidence you have, such as photographs of injuries, damaged property, or any written communication from the abuser. These pieces of evidence can strengthen your case if legal action is taken.

3. Police Reports: After responding to the incident, the police will usually file a report. Request a copy of this report for your records, as it will be essential in legal proceedings, obtaining a restraining order, or seeking support services.

4. Requesting a Restraining Order: If you feel unsafe or fear future harm, consider requesting a restraining order against your partner as soon as possible. The police report can serve as valuable evidence to support your request. Reach out to the court or local authorities to begin the process and get guidance on the necessary steps.

5. Legal Proceedings: If you decide to press charges or pursue legal action against your partner, cooperate fully with the authorities and legal system. Be prepared to

testify if needed and provide any additional evidence requested.

6. Safety Planning: While law enforcement can provide immediate assistance during emergencies, it's essential to have a comprehensive safety plan in place for long-term protection. Collaborate with advocates, support organizations, or counselors to develop a plan tailored to your unique situation.

7. Know Your Rights: Familiarize yourself with your rights as a survivor of domestic abuse. Many countries have laws and protections in place for victims, such as victim compensation programs, legal assistance, and access to support services.

8. Seeking Support: Engage with local domestic violence organizations or helplines. They can provide guidance, emotional support, and resources to help you navigate the legal process and rebuild your life.

CUSTODY AND DIVORCE CONSIDERATIONS

Custody involves two aspects. The first is physical custody, which refers to where the child lives and the time spent with each parent, commonly known as parenting time. The second aspect is legal custody, granting the right to make significant decisions concerning the child's education, medical care, religion, etc.

When legal professionals discuss custody, they typically refer to legal custody. In many cases, joint legal custody (50/50) is the standard unless there are substantial issues.

Parenting time or physical custody is what most people commonly think of when discussing custody. If one parent has the children most of the time and the other has visitation rights, they may be referred to as the primary custodian. However, it's important to note that they usually still share joint physical custody, even if the time is not equally divided. The approach to parenting time can vary from state to state, with some advocating strongly for equal time while others may not. This might seem cruel but it is not.

REASONS WHY PEOPLE STAY IN ABUSIVE RELATIONSHIPS

1. Kids: Sometimes, I get questions such as "Is it ok for a woman to stay in an abusive marriage because of the kids?" a very simple question that deserves a simple answer, NO! It's not worth it. To be honest, staying in an abusive relationship can have detrimental effects on your

children. By remaining in such a situation, you are inadvertently setting a harmful pattern for their future relationships. Your daughters may learn that it's acceptable for a man to mistreat and hurt them, both physically and emotionally. Similarly, your sons may absorb the message that it's appropriate to treat women poorly. These patterns are not healthy, and it's crucial to break this cycle.

You deserve to be safe and happy, and the same applies to your children. They deserve to witness healthy, respectful relationships and expect the same from their future partners. Leaving an abusive relationship sets an essential example for your children and helps create a healthier environment for their emotional and psychological well-being. Prioritizing safety and well-being not only benefits you but also positively influences your children's future experiences and relationships.

2. Finance: What are my options? I have no money, no car, nothing. How can I leave an abusive relationship? Almost every person in an abusive relationship has become dependent on the abuser. It's a trick they use to control you. Once they have you totally dependent on them, they can treat you anyway they want and they know that you will allow their terrible behavior because

you can't leave. They isolate you from friends and family so you won't have someone save you.

In your local area, you can find valuable resources for individuals seeking help from abusive relationships. Use a search engine like Google to look up terms such as "domestic violence shelter [your city name]" to discover available options. When reaching out, ensure you use a safe phone line that your abuser cannot access and seek assistance from these organizations to create a plan.

Considering your social anxiety, it may feel daunting to contact unfamiliar individuals, but muster your strength to overcome the fear and make that call. Once you take that courageous step, the process will become more manageable, and the support you receive will make a significant difference.

3. Fear of Consequences: The person may fear what will happen if they leave the relationship, such as retaliation or further harm.

4. Lack of Awareness: Some individuals may not recognize that their relationship is unhealthy because they grew up in an environment where abuse was common, and they don't know what a healthy relationship looks like.

5. Fear of Disclosure: If someone is in an LGBTQ relationship and hasn't come out to everyone, their partner may threaten to reveal this secret, leading to fear and vulnerability.

6. Embarrassment and Shame: Admitting abuse can be challenging due to feelings of shame and worry about how others will judge them.

7. Low Self-Esteem: Constant put-downs and blame from the abusive partner may lead the victim to believe they are at fault for the abuse.

8. Conflicting Emotions: Despite the abuse, the victim may still have feelings of love for their partner, especially if they have children together and wish to maintain their family.

9. Cultural or Religious Influences: Traditional gender roles or cultural norms may pressure the person to stay in the relationship to avoid bringing shame upon their family.

10. Language Barriers and Immigration Status: Language barriers and fear of affecting immigration status can hinder communication and reporting the abuse.

11. Disability and Dependency: Physical dependence on the abusive partner can create a belief that their well-being is tied to the relationship, leading to difficulty leaving.

Based on my observations, many individuals in abusive relationships do not stay because they enjoy it; rather, it's often due to the lack of better options. Leaving can be frightening, especially when one is financially dependent on the abuser, worried about the safety of their children, or fearful of the abuser's potential for serious violence. This fear is further heightened for those who grew up in abusive or neglectful environments, lacking emotional resources or a support system to rely on.

It's disheartening to hear insensitive remarks like, "She can just walk away anytime she wants," as it ignores the complexities and challenges faced by abuse victims. Such comments blame the victim, and it frustrates me to see these responses from people. Empathy and understanding are essential when discussing these sensitive issues.

After all said and done, I highly recommend divorce in any case of domestic abuse. Stop thinking you can save the relationship, abusers don't change, you will end up totally drained with nowhere to turn to.

The best time to leave an abuser is yesterday, the next best time is now.

CONSIDERATIONS IN DIVORCE

visiting rights: on the ground that you have evaluate your spouse and they are not terrible fathers, you can arrange visiting time for them with the kids, but if they have acted abusive towards the children in your presence or that you have knowledge of, better get evidence and deny them visiting rights or only grand supervised visiting rights so they kids don't go unsupervised when with them. this will save you a lot of heart ache.

Child support: your partner should be responsible enough to pay child which will be mandated of them by the court. If they fail to do so due to reasons beyond their control, you might grant them a little consideration but it should have it's limit. Know when to be firm and when to be lenient.

Abusers hate to lose their victim, it simply means lack of control for them hence they will do anything possible to get their victim back which might include apologizing and acting all nice and playing the repented perfect spouse.

Do not be deceived, your worse mistake will be to go back to them, many have lost their lives by retuning to abusive relationships.

CHAPTER FIVE

NAVIGATING EMOTIONAL CHALLENGES

WHAT CHANGES WHEN YOU FINALLY LEAVE AN ABUSIVE RELATIONSHIP

At the beginning, it's a painful and miserable experience. Over time, you start to miss the abuse, not because you want it, but because any form of attention seems better than feeling empty.

It becomes routine, and though you've broken free, you still feel scared and trapped. True freedom feels elusive, and the path to it is often overlooked.

Leaving an abusive partner involves an internal battle every day. Your mind may downplay the abuse, while your broken heart craves their presence despite the pain.

When your mind and heart unite against you, enticing you back, the fight intensifies. Your abuser's influence may linger in your thoughts, making you feel unlovable and alone.

After enduring this struggle, true change begins. The pain gradually subsides, and you focus on self-improvement. You embrace and nurture the wounded inner child within you, realizing that you deserve better.

You decide to try harder, rebuild your heart, and retrain your brain. Slowly, the painful memories become distant and less piercing. Hurtful words lose their power, and the physical scars fade.

Finally, you discover the freedom to be yourself, the person you always deserved to be. You embrace a new beginning, planting a garden of positivity and growth in your life.

COPING WITH GUILT AND SHAME

Feeling guilty in an abusive relationship can result from manipulation and conditioning by the abuser, along with your empathetic and caring nature. The years spent with the abuser create strong memories that are hard to forget, contributing to the guilt.

Leaving an abusive partner often means stepping out of your comfort zone, especially if you were made dependent on them. Embracing this new independence can be challenging and frightening, making the mind seek the safety of the comfort zone and triggering feelings of guilt.

Abusers tend to shift blame onto their victims, claiming that the victim's actions or words provoked the abusive behavior. They avoid taking responsibility for the failing relationship and portray themselves as innocent unless provoked by the victim.
They have a deep understanding of your vulnerabilities and can manipulate their words to make you question your sanity, making you feel like the crazy one, while portraying themselves as the victim.

Although it's challenging, if you truly want to overcome these feelings, I recommend taking positive steps: engage in activities that bring you joy, celebrate small achievements, build a strong support system with friends and family, reconnect with loved ones, and try to avoid confrontations with the abuser. If unavoidable, always have a third party present.

Exploring new hobbies or revisiting old ones, reading books, and enjoying outdoor activities like swimming, biking, hiking, or nature walks can be uplifting and empowering.

Remember, breaking free from the abusive relationship is beneficial for you and even for the abuser. Your best days lie ahead, and only you have the power to shape them. Let go of the guilt and embrace a brighter future.

HEALING FROM TRAUMA

Leaving an abusive relationship is a significant step, and now it's essential to focus on healing and self-care.

Recovering from an abusive relationship may evoke intense emotions, and it's essential to recognize that all these feelings are valid and part of the healing process.

You may experience various thoughts and feelings, such as missing your ex, feeling lonely, or even considering going back to the relationship. It's normal to feel uncertain or struggle with making decisions on your own, and you might find it challenging to feel independent.

Feelings of anxiety, depression, or fear of danger may also arise, and some survivors may experience symptoms of post-traumatic stress disorder (PTSD).

On the other hand, there may be positive emotions too. You might feel a sense of freedom and relief, as if a heavy burden has been lifted.

Throughout the healing journey, you may have both good and bad days, feeling strong and confident on some days and overwhelmed with sadness and doubt on others. Remember that all these emotions are entirely normal, and it's crucial to be patient and compassionate with yourself as you navigate this process.
After leaving an abusive relationship, healing may not be the immediate focus, as survival becomes a priority, according to Gross.

The time it takes to heal varies for each survivor since everyone's experience is unique.

However, the important aspect is the potential for healing, the possibility to reach a point where you can recognize, understand, and respond appropriately to your triggers.

BUILDING SELF-ESTEEM AND CONFIDENCE

A toxic relationship can have a more profound impact on mental and emotional well-being than just physical health. It may lead to anxiety, depression, low self-esteem, and insecurities, affecting not only current relationships but also future ones with family and friends.

However, it is possible to rebuild self-esteem after a toxic relationship. While it won't happen overnight, taking small steps over time can lead to a stronger and better version of yourself physically, mentally, emotionally, and spiritually.

To start the journey of self-improvement, you can identify toxic beliefs about yourself and change the narrative. Recognize negative thoughts originating from others' hurtful words and replace them with positive affirmations. Practice writing down negative beliefs and rewriting them as constructive affirmations to reinforce throughout the day.

1. List your positive attributes, as toxic people's hurtful behavior might make you forget your strengths. Remind yourself of your past successes and qualities, such as intelligence, quick learning, or excellent people skills, to regain confidence in yourself. Embrace the process with patience and kindness towards yourself as you rediscover and reaffirm your true identity.

2. Establish clear boundaries in all future relationships after cutting ties with toxic ones. Identify non-negotiables for you in a relationship and prioritize your needs. Toxic people often

disregard boundaries, so defining them is crucial
for maintaining healthy connections.

3. Nurture healthy relationships by building a strong
    support system with family or close friends who
    will be honest and supportive. Spending time with
    caring individuals who want to see you thrive will
    boost your self-esteem and sense of belonging.

4. Take care of your physical health, which may have
    suffered during the draining effects of an
    unhealthy relationship. Schedule annual check-ups,
    assess your diet, and incorporate exercise to live a
    fuller life.

5. Prioritize self-care and dedicate time to activities
    that rejuvenate you, such as journaling, reading, or
    engaging in hobbies. Remember that self-care is
    essential for your well-being and not a selfish act.

6. Declutter your environment to create a clutter-free
    space that promotes a clearer mind and reduces
    stress. Taking small steps to declutter gradually
    will lead to a fresh start and a calmer mind.

7. Step back from social media, as it can steal your
    joy by promoting unrealistic comparisons and
    negative comments. Remember that most people

present edited versions of their lives, not showing
the challenges they face.

8. Set achievable goals to boost your self-esteem.
    Create a list of short and long-term objectives for
    different aspects of your life, focusing on spiritual,
    family, relationship, financial, and health goals.

9. Turn to the Bible for uplifting and empowering
    words. Pray and ask God for guidance and
    wisdom, and seek passages that resonate with your
    current life situation.

Take it one step at a time and slowly implement these
self-esteem-building practices. By recreating your life
with positive changes, you'll notice improvements in
your self-esteem and self-worth.

CHAPTER SIX

FINANCIAL INDEPENDENCE

While economic or financial abuse might not be the main topic of discussions concerning abusive relationships, it is surprisingly prevalent. In fact, it occurs in 99 percent of abusive relationships and is a significant factor that can lead you to remain in or return to such situations. The repercussions of financial abuse are long-lasting and can affect various aspects of your life, hindering your ability to move forward.

Achieving financial independence, particularly after experiencing abuse, is a gradual process. To regain control of your finances, it is essential to dedicate time to educate yourself on financial planning and related topics. Once you are in a safe environment and have been able to find a source of income, no matter how little, the next question is "what comes next?" This next chapter can be overwhelming cause at this point, all you want to do is relax from the after effect of leaving an abusive relationship but this is actually an opportunity to lay a strong foundation for the next chapter of your life. The following are steps you can to establish your financial independence and ensure long term financial strength

OPEN AN ACCOUNT

Begin by opening a bank account and initiating your savings journey. While it's ideal to open an account while planning your escape, not everyone has that luxury. Nonetheless, having a secure source of money is the first step towards achieving financial independence.

1. Select a reputable bank that suits your needs. Some banks offer in-person budgeting assistance, while others have convenient online financial management options. National banks offer a broader range of services, while local banks or credit unions offer a personal touch. Do your research and seek recommendations from friends or family. Be mindful of the associated fees. The process of opening a bank account is generally straightforward. You'll need your Social Security number and a valid ID. Some banks may require minimum deposits for specific account types. If possible, open both checking and savings accounts and begin saving whenever you can.

2. Prioritize saving a portion of every paycheck for an emergency fund. Experts recommend allocating 20 percent of your paycheck to savings, but start with what you can manage. Not having funds for

unexpected expenses can significantly impact your finances and lead to debt.

3. Strive to build an emergency fund that covers at least three to six months' worth of essential expenses. Once you achieve that, consider saving for other financial goals like vacations, education, or a house deposit, or even investing for retirement.

4. Create a budget that suits your needs once your account is set up. This will help you track where your money is spent.

5. During the initial months after leaving, putting food on the table might be challenging. Look for local food banks in your area or use Feeding America's search tool to find assistance.

6. Federal benefit programs are available to support qualifying individuals and families after leaving an abusive situation. These programs can help with groceries, healthcare, housing, and more, including non-cash benefits like childcare and job training.

7. Domestic abuse coalitions in various states offer support to survivors, assisting with rejoining the

workforce, connecting with other survivors, and finding support groups.

Recovering financially and emotionally after abuse is a gradual process. Celebrate every step towards financial stability to avoid discouragement.

This chapter of your life may be filled with a mix of emotions, but never give up. Rebuilding your financial health is a lifelong journey, so take it one step at a time.

CHAPTER SEVEN

PROTECTING CHILDREN FROM VIOLENCE

EXPLAINING DOMESTIC VIOLENCE TO CHILDREN

When domestic violence survivors decide to end an abusive relationship, it often involves going through a divorce, which can be challenging, especially when children are involved. Knowing how to talk to kids about this significant change after enduring trauma can be tough. Here are some steps to start this difficult conversation:

1. Begin with the Truth:
- Be honest with your children in a way they can understand, as it helps them feel safer in the long run.
- Children are more aware of domestic violence than we might think, even if they don't fully understand it.
- Explain that abuse is a choice made by the abusive parent, and this is why you've chosen to live separately.

- Reassure children that it's okay to have conflicting feelings, including love for the abusive parent.
- Professional counseling may be beneficial for both the protective parent and children to navigate the complex emotions after domestic violence.

2. Prepare the Child for Changes:
- Break down the conversation into several points, explaining what divorce means.
- Emphasize that the divorce is not the child's fault and reassure them of your love.
- Discuss how certain aspects of the family will change, like a parent living elsewhere, while reassuring them about stability in other areas (e.g., school, friends, extended family, pets).
- Prepare them for the amount of time they might spend with the other parent.
- Allow them to ask questions and be honest if there's a protection order in place, explaining that it's for their safety.

Anticipate resistance and confusion from your children during this challenging period. They might not grasp the reasons behind the divorce or protection order and could exhibit anger towards the protective parent. Understand that this reaction is their way of coping with trauma and change, so don't take it personally. Maintain healthy boundaries and suggest other outlets for them to express their emotions, like writing, drawing, or confiding in someone they trust (a friend, grandparent, school counselor, etc.). Be patient during this process as it is crucial for their well-being.

CO-PARENTING WITH AN ABUSIVE PARTNER

Co-parenting with an abusive partner will only be possible if the abuse have never involved the kids. If your ex-partner has been abusive towards the kids in the past, talk to your attorney for other options.

1. Setting a positive example for your kids is crucial, and you must not tolerate any bullying, abuse, or harassment.

2. Avoid getting entangled in your ex-partner's verbal games.

3. Keep your personal conflicts separate from the kids, and focus on their well-being.

4. While co-parenting with an abusive ex may be necessary, it's essential to involve a neutral third party who can handle drop-offs, pickups, and supervise interactions. The third party should be chosen by you alone.

5. For emergencies, communicate via text and ensure your ex-partner is not allowed near your home or be with the kids unsupervised to prevent further harm.

CHAPTER EIGHT

REBUILDING YOUR LIFE AFTER LEAVING

SETTING BOUNDARIES AND HEALTHY RELATIONSHIP

Rebuilding your life after leaving an abusive relationship is a challenging and transformative process that requires time, effort, and a commitment to self-healing. One of the critical aspects of this journey is setting boundaries and establishing healthy relationships.

1. Understanding the Importance of Boundaries:
Setting boundaries is fundamental to maintaining your emotional and physical well-being. After experiencing abuse, your sense of self-worth and personal boundaries may have been eroded. Recognizing the need for boundaries allows you to reclaim control over your life and protect yourself from future harm.

2. Identifying Your Boundaries:
Start by identifying your boundaries and values. Reflect on what behaviors are acceptable to you and what crosses the line. This includes defining limits on communication, personal space, emotional intimacy, and respect in

relationships. Knowing your boundaries will help you communicate them clearly to others.

3. Communicating Boundaries:

Learning to communicate your boundaries assertively is crucial. Practice expressing your needs and limits with confidence and clarity. Being open about your boundaries ensures that others are aware of your expectations, and it sets the foundation for healthy relationships.

4. Recognizing Red Flags:

Having experienced an abusive relationship, it's essential to recognize red flags in potential partners or friends. Trust your intuition and be cautious of anyone who shows signs of controlling behavior, manipulation, or disrespect. Surround yourself with people who support your growth and respect your boundaries.

5. Seeking Support and Therapy:

Rebuilding your life after abuse can be emotionally overwhelming. Consider seeking support from friends, family, or support groups. Professional therapy can also be instrumental in helping you process trauma, rebuild self-esteem, and develop healthier relationship patterns.

6. Prioritizing Self-Care:

Taking care of yourself is crucial during this healing process. Engage in self-care practices that nourish your mind, body, and soul. This may include exercise, mindfulness, journaling, or pursuing hobbies that bring you joy.

7. Learning from Past Mistakes:
Reflect on your past relationship and understand the patterns that led to abuse. Acknowledge any role you might have played in enabling the abusive behavior and use this self-awareness to prevent repeating the same mistakes in the future.

8. Taking Relationships Slowly:
As you venture into new relationships, take things slowly and avoid rushing into commitment. Allow yourself time to build trust and assess whether the person respects your boundaries and treats you with kindness and understanding.

9. Forgiving Yourself and Letting Go:
Healing from an abusive relationship involves forgiving yourself for any perceived shortcomings and letting go of guilt or shame. Remember that you are not defined by your past and that you deserve to be treated with love and respect.

10. Celebrating Progress:
Celebrate your progress and small victories along the
way. Recognize the strength it takes to rebuild your life
after leaving an abusive relationship. Acknowledge your
growth and resilience as you work towards creating a
new and healthier future.

In summary, rebuilding your life after leaving an abusive
relationship involves setting and communicating
boundaries, recognizing red flags, seeking support,
prioritizing self-care, and learning from the past.
Embrace this journey of healing, self-discovery, and
growth as you pave the way towards healthier
relationships and a brighter future.

CONCLUSION

Experiencing abuse, whether physical or psychological, not only increases the likelihood of developing mental health issues but also significantly affects various aspects of our lives, including our self-perception and personality. Such exposure has been found to have a detrimental impact on our overall well-being and how we view ourselves.

It is therefore of utmost importance that we protect ourselves and avoid abusive relationships as much as we can, but in the event that we find ourselves in such situations, it is also important that we understand the behavioral pattern of abusers and the various faces of abuse.

Healing and recovering from an abusive or toxic relationship can be a challenging journey, but it is a crucial step towards reclaiming your life and finding a sense of freedom and empowerment. It's essential to acknowledge the range of emotions you may experience, from fear and uncertainty to hope and strength.

Remember that healing is a unique process, and there is no set time frame for it. Building self-esteem after leaving such a relationship requires patience, self-compassion, and dedication to personal growth.

Creating boundaries, nurturing healthy relationships, taking care of your body, practicing self-care, and decluttering your environment are all essential steps in rebuilding your self-esteem and rediscovering your worth. Additionally, setting achievable goals and seeking guidance from God's word can provide valuable support on this journey of healing.

While it may feel overwhelming at times, remember that you are not alone, and seeking support from friends, family, or professional resources can be instrumental in your healing process. Embrace the possibility of growth and transformation, and know that you have the strength within you to create a brighter future filled with self-love and genuine happiness. As you navigate this path of healing, remember to be kind to yourself and celebrate the progress you make, no matter how small. Your best days are ahead, and you have the power to shape them into what you truly desire.

www.ingramcontent.com/pod-product-compliance
Lightning Source LLC
Chambersburg PA
CBHW070958250726
48663CB00002B/276